HAVE A NICE DAY!

A Play by Steve Barlow and Steve Skidmore

Series Editors: Steve Barlow and Steve Skidmore

Heinemann

Published by Heinemann Educational Publishers
Halley Court, Jordan Hill, Oxford OX2 8EJ
A division of Reed Educational and Professional Publishing Ltd

OXFORD   MELBOURNE   AUCKLAND
JOHANNESBURG   BLANTYRE   GABORONE
IBADAN   PORTSMOUTH NH (USA)   CHICAGO

© Steve Barlow and Steve Skidmore, 2001
Original illustrations © Heinemann Educational Publishers 2001

All rights reserved. No part of this publication may be reproduced in any material form (including photocopying or storing it in any medium by electronic means and whether or not transiently or incidentally to some other use of this publication) without the prior written permission of the copyright owner, except in accordance with the provisions of the Copyright, Designs and Patents Act 1988 or under the terms of a licence issued by the Copyright Licensing Agency Ltd, 90 Tottenham Court Road, London W1P 9HE. Applications for the copyright owner's written permission to reproduce any part of this publication should be addressed in the first instance to the publisher.

First published 2001
05 04 03 02 01
10 9 8 7 6 5 4 3 2 1
ISBN 0 435 212885

Illustrations by Carlos Pino
Cover design by Shireen Nathoo Design
Cover artwork by Bob Lea
Designed by Artistix, Thame, Oxon
Printed and bound in Great Britain by Biddles Ltd

Tel: 01865 888058 www.heinemann.co.uk

Contents

Characters	4
Scene One	6
Scene Two	17
Scene Three	27

Characters

Mr Moody is the manager of the Happy Burger restaurant. He is very keen to impress head office.

Jaz is 18. This is his first job since leaving school, and he hates it. He just likes drawing, but who will pay him to do that?

Janice is in her thirties. Without her cheerful common sense, the restaurant would soon fall to pieces.

Jo is 18, and she works with Jaz and Janice in the restaurant. She dreams of meeting Mr Right.

Dave Best used to be the college heart-throb. His life has changed a lot since those days.

Monica is Jo's friend. She needs a job, but does the Happy Burger need her?

SCENE ONE

The kitchen of a Happy Burgers fast-food restaurant, somewhere in England. Morning.

MOODY: *(With a big smile)* Have a nice day!

JAZ: *(Sulky)* Have a nice day.

MOODY: No, no. *(With a bigger smile)* Have a nice day!

JAZ: *(Still sulky)* Have a nice day.

MOODY: Oh, for pity's sake – can't you just make an effort? You've got to make your customers feel that you really want them to have a nice day.

(Janice comes in from the restaurant.)

JANICE: Is anything wrong, Mr Moody?

MOODY: I just want him to say 'Have a nice day' as if he means it. He says it as if he hopes all the customers will fall under a bus. *(To Jaz)* Try it again. 'Have a nice day!'

JAZ: What if somebody's died?

MOODY: What?

JAZ: Well, I don't know, do I? If I say 'Have a nice day' to someone and they say 'Me gran's just died,' I'll look a right plank.

MOODY: Look, somebody whose gran's just died isn't going to come in here for burgers, are they?

JAZ: That lot did last week. Straight from the crematorium. They said the Dog and Duck was too expensive. I served 'em fourteen Happy Meals.

7

JANICE: That's right. I remember they complained because you'd burnt the fries.

JAZ: Yeah, and I said *(he sniggers)* I said, I bet they're not as burnt as...

JANICE: Yes, all right, Jaz. Mr Moody doesn't want to hear about all that. Why don't you go and wipe some tables?

(Jaz heads for the door leading to the tables.)

MOODY: Aren't you forgetting something? What do we never do?

JAZ: Spit in the burgers?

MOODY: Apart from that! *(Jaz looks blank)* We never go anywhere empty-handed.

(Jaz looks around. He takes the lid off a waste bin and heads for the restaurant, carrying the lid like a shield.)

JANICE: Jaz!

(Jaz traipses back to Janice. She takes the lid off him and gives him a cloth and a spray bottle.)

JANICE: Tables. Wipe.

(Jaz goes out. Janice and Mr Moody watch him.)

MOODY: Tell me, Janice. How long does it normally take Happy Burger workers to get their Gold Badge?

JANICE: Two or three weeks.

MOODY: And how long has Jaz been working towards his?

JANICE: Eighteen months.

(The back door flies open. Jo rushes in.)

MOODY: At last! Do you know what time it is?

JO: Sorry, Mr Moody. I had to take my little sister to playgroup and the bus was late and...

MOODY: I don't want to know! This is a very important week for me. John P Rottenburger The Third has flown over from America to visit Happy Burgers outlets. He is coming here on Saturday.

JO: Oh yeah – for your Fun Day thingy!

MOODY: I want Mr Rottenburger to see a clean, well-run branch of Happy Burgers greeting customers with a big smile. Just remember, Jo – 'A day without a burger is a day without sunshine.'

JO: That's in the training book, isn't it?

MOODY: Yes, and what other slogans are in there?

JO: Er ... 'Give me a Happy and make it snappy!' Er ...

JANICE: *(Reminding Jo)* 'We're a bunch of Happy Burgers.'

JO: Yeah – hey, I've got a good one – 'If a burger ain't Happy, it must taste cr...'

MOODY: *(Cutting her off)* Just stick to the script, Jo. All right?

And clean yourself up before a customer sees you – you look like something the cat brought in.

(Jaz wanders in carrying a pot plant.)

JANICE: Jaz, where are you going with that?

JAZ: Moody said, 'Never go anywhere empty-handed.'

MOODY: Oh, for crying out loud – you take something that belongs in the restaurant. You *bring back* something that belongs in the kitchen.

JAZ: You never said.

MOODY: Why do I employ you?

JAZ: Because you can't get anybody else to work here, and I'm cheap.

MOODY: Saturday is the most important day of my life, and who have I got to rely on? Dumb and Dumber.

(Moody storms off into the restaurant.)

JO: What's up with him?

JANICE: He's set his heart on getting a Pink Flag.

JO: What's that?

JANICE: The Crew of the Month award. Everybody gets a bonus. Mr Moody's hoping Mr Rottenburger will be so impressed with his Happy Day, we'll win it.

JO: Cool! I could do with a bonus.

JANICE: We're getting a Mister Happy from head office. You know, some bloke in a foam rubber costume.

(Jaz pulls a paper napkin out of his pocket and begins to draw.)

JO: And balloons?

JANICE: And a bouncy castle.

JO: So what happens when all the kids have stuffed themselves with burgers and then go bouncing about on the castle?

JANICE: I don't think Mr Moody's thought of that.

JAZ: I bet I have to clean it up.

JANICE: By the way, have you filled in your competition form yet?

JO: What form's that?

(Janice takes a printed form out of her pocket and gives it to Jo.)

JANICE: You've got to suggest a name for our new line – kangaroo burgers. And a new slogan for the ad.

JO: Yeah, all right then. Should be a laugh.

(Jo fills in her form. Janice gets busy in the kitchen. Jo looks over at what Jaz is drawing.)

JO: Hey, that looks good. Let's have a look.

JAZ: It's only a drawing.

JO: *(Holding it up)* You've drawn Mister Happy. Wow, that's brilliant! Did you learn to draw like that at school?

JAZ: I was useless at school. I can't do nothin'. Why d'you think I'm workin' here?

JO: But this drawing's really good!

JAZ: It's only a drawing. It's not like bein' good at maths or science. You can't get a job just drawing. The careers teacher said.

(A buzzer goes. Janice goes towards the counter.)

JO: Can I go, Janice? I've got my counter star, look!

(She proudly displays the star on her gold badge.)

JANICE: Go on, then.

JO: *(Jo goes to the counter. To a customer offstage:)* Welcome to Happy Burgers. My name's Jo. How can I help you?

DAVE BEST: *(Offstage)* I'll have a Happy Burger without gherkins, please.

JO: *(Very loudly)* One lump of fat in a bun, hold the slugs!

JANICE: *(Busy at the grill)* Nice one, Jo. Very professional.

JO: If you'd like to take a seat, your order will be with you shortly. Have a nice day! *(She turns from the counter and runs across to Janice)* Do you know who that was?

12

JANICE: No, who?

JO: Dave Best!

JANICE: Who?

JO: He was at my college last year. He was dead popular – all the girls fancied him.

JANICE: Oh. *(To Jaz)* Make yourself useful. Take this order.

(Sighing, Jaz takes the burger and fries into the restaurant.)

JO: He's drop dead gorgeous.

(From the restaurant comes the sound of a chair tipping over.)

DAVE BEST: *(Offstage)* You idiot! Look at this mess.

JAZ: *(Offstage)* Sorry.

(Jaz comes in.)

JANICE: What happened?

JAZ: It wasn't my fault. I was givin' him his burger, only the top came open and it fell out. He's got mayo all over his Levis.

(Mr Moody leads Dave Best into the kitchen.)

MOODY: I am so sorry, sir. One of our staff will help you clean up. I hope you'll accept a full refund and a free Happy Meal. *(To Jaz, angrily)* Go away!

(Jaz goes out of the door at the back of the kitchen.)

DAVE BEST: That's okay. No, really, if I could just have a cloth ... *(He spots Jo)* Jean!

JO: Jo.

DAVE BEST: That's right, Jo! I didn't know you worked here.

JO: I've just started.

DAVE BEST: Great! Hang on a minute, I just need to make an urgent call. *(He takes out a mobile phone and flips it open)* Hi, Larry? Listen, about the Nike account ...

JANICE: Here's a cloth.

JO: I'll do it!

JANICE: Down, girl. He can do it himself.

DAVE BEST: *(On phone)* Tell Tiger it's a hundred million or no deal, and I'm not giving him any more free golf lessons, okay? ... Great. Have your people talk to his people and get back to my people. Ciao.

(He switches off the phone and wipes his trousers.)

JO: Are you talking about that golfer ... ?

DAVE BEST: Ah – you didn't hear anything, okay? You've got to be careful in advertising.

JO: Ooh, are you in advertising? You must be doing ever so well.

DAVE BEST: You know how it is. Can't complain. Hey, are you doing anything tonight?

JO: No.

DAVE BEST: Well, you are now. I'll pick you up at six, okay?

(Dave Best throws the cloth back to Jo and goes out. The phone in Mr Moody's office rings. He goes to answer it.)

JAZ: *(Coming back in)* Hey, look what I found!

(He holds up a mousetrap with half a mouse dangling from it.)

JO: Oh, that is so gross.

JANICE: Where's the other half? *(Jaz shrugs)* Oh well, I suppose it'll turn up sooner or later.

(Mr Moody comes back from taking the call.)

MOODY: That was Debbie. She says she's got flu. She'll be off for a week. What am I going to do? It's Happy Day tomorrow, and we're short-handed as it is.

JO: Mr Moody! I've got a friend who could help out. She's worked for MacWimpey's.

MOODY: Well, I don't know ... oh, I suppose so. Just make sure you're both here on time. We can't afford to upset Mr Rottenburger.

JO: Yes, Mr Moody.

MOODY: This Fun Day could make or break my whole career. I want that Pink Flag! So tomorrow, we will be a team. We are Happy Burgers.

**JO,
JANICE &
JAZ:** *(Together)* Yes, Mr Moody.

MOODY: And don't you dare forget it!

Scene Two

Inside the restaurant, next day. Mr Moody is speaking into a phone.

17

MOODY: *(Into phone)* Yes, Mr Rottenburger … No, Mr Rottenburger … Of course, Mr Rottenburger … See you later, Mr Rottenburger. *(He flicks the phone shut)* That was Mr Rottenburger.

JANICE: You don't say.

MOODY: He's just set off from head office. He'll be here soon. Then it's Crew of the Month and Pink Flags all round! Is everything ready?

JANICE: As ready as it will ever be.

(Mr Moody reads from a clipboard.)

MOODY: Happy balloons – check. Bouncy castle – check. Happy banners …

(He looks up at a banner hanging over the door and sighs.)

MOODY: Did Jaz do that?

JANICE: *(Nodding)* Jaz did that.

MOODY: *(Shouting)* Jaz! Get here now!

(Jaz hurries out of the kitchen.)

MOODY: Jaz, how many 'G's are there in 'burgers'?

JAZ: Four?

MOODY: Not even close. And there are two 'R's. Take it down.

(Jaz begins to do so as Jo enters with Monica.)

MOODY: *(To Jo)* You're late again.

JO: Sorry. I'm in love.

MOODY: So why does that make you late?

JO: Time stands still when you're in love.

JANICE: Jaz must be in love all the time, then.

MOODY: There's no time for love in the fast-food business.

JO: You just don't understand.

MOODY: I understand this. If you're late again, you're sacked. *(He points at Monica)* Who's she?

JO: This is Monica. The person I told you about.

MONICA: *(Bored)* Hi.

MOODY: Hello, Monica, welcome aboard. Today's a big day for us here. I need you to wipe tables and take food out to the customers. Can you manage that, love?

MONICA: *(Sarcastically)* Just about. Luckily, I'm studying 'A' Level Table Wiping at college.

MOODY: You'll be paid by the minute, and at the end of the shift you can have a Woppa Happy burger.

MONICA: I don't eat meat. I'm a vegetarian.

MOODY: Well, you can have a veggie-burger, instead.

MONICA: No thanks. I hate burgers. Burger bars like this are destroying the world.

MOODY: Are they really? So why are you here?

MONICA: I need the cash.

MOODY: Well, you can save the world on your time, love. On my time, you wipe tables. And remember to put on a happy face. Let me see those teeth!
Think H-A-P-P-Y. Big smile, big grin.

MONICA: *(Under her breath)* Big prat.

MOODY: I'm going to see where Mr Happy has got to.

(He goes out the door. Jaz takes the banner back to the kitchen.)

JANICE: *(To Jo)* So, you went out with Dave Best?

JO: Yes, he's wonderful. A real success story. He took me to a Turkish restaurant.

MONICA: You mean a kebab house.

JO: Well, yeah. But it was dead romantic.

(Mr Moody enters with Mr Happy. Mr Happy is a green and yellow character made from foam. He bounces around the tables.)

MR HAPPY: Happy, happy, happy!

JANICE: I don't believe this.

JO: Oh, isn't he cute?

MR HAPPY: Happy, happy, happy!

MOODY: *(To Monica)* Why are you standing around? I need you to get wiping, love.

MONICA: I need you to stop calling me 'love'.

MOODY: Oh, do you? You're working for me now, *love*. I'll call you what I want.

MONICA: Oh, will you? Right, then.

(Monica moves over to a customer. He is happily eating a burger.)

MONICA: Are you enjoying that burger?

(The customer nods.)

MONICA: Most of that burger is made out of offal. Do you know what offal is?

(The customer shakes his head.)

MONICA: Shall I tell you?

(Monica whispers in the customer's ear. He looks shaken and then looks at his burger. He puts his hand over his mouth and runs towards the toilet.)

MONICA: Have a nice day!

MR HAPPY: Happy, happy, happy!

(Mr Moody goes over to Monica.)

MOODY: What's the matter with him?

MONICA: He ate something that disagreed with him. *Love*.

21

MOODY: Get wiping! The tables must be spotless for Mr Rottenburger.

(Monica moves towards another table and talks to another customer.)

MONICA: Mmm. Chicken burgers! It's ever so clever, how they make them.

(The customer looks up. Monica carries on telling the customer how chicken burgers are made, miming all the horrible bits. The customer looks more and more upset. More customers start to listen.)

MOODY: *(To Janice)* We don't want customers being ill, while Mr Rottenburger's here.

JANICE: Calm down, Mr Moody. Have you had your pills?

(Monica finishes telling the customers about chicken burgers.)

MONICA: And then you eat it. Isn't that amazing!

(The customers drop their food and rush out.)

(Mr Moody tries to stop them.)

MOODY: Where are you going? Come back! Please!

MR HAPPY: Happy, happy, happy!

(Mr Moody turns to Monica.)

MOODY: What have you done?

MONICA: I'm just telling the customers how burgers are made.

MOODY: They don't want to know that. It'll upset them.

MONICA: But I'm just being truthful.

MOODY: Grow up, love. This is business! Telling the truth isn't going to win us Crew of the Month.

(One of the customers screams.)

MOODY: Now what?

(Mr Moody rushes over to find out what is wrong. Monica follows.)

MOODY: Oh no! I'm terribly sorry, sir, I don't know how this can have happened ...

(Monica picks up a burger from the customer's plate. There is half a mouse inside the bun. She holds the bun up.)

MONICA: *(Very loudly)* Oh look, Mr Moody, there's half a mouse inside this bun!

MOODY: Ssssh!

JAZ: I wondered where that had got to!

JANICE: That's the first time there's been real meat in a Happy Burger.

MONICA: *(To another customer)* You can see its little whiskers, look!

MOODY: Will you be quiet!

(All the rest of the customers get up and leave.)

MOODY: No, don't go! What will Mr Rottenburger say?

MR HAPPY: Happy, happy, happy!

MOODY: *(To Monica)* This is all your fault! You're sacked!

MONICA: That's not fair! I didn't put the mouse in the burger!

MR HAPPY: Happy, happy, happy!

MONICA: You can shut up, as well! If you're so keen on burgers, eat this!

(Monica rams the mouse-burger into Mr Happy's rubber mouth and runs into the kitchen.)

MR HAPPY: Aarrgghh! I've got pickle in my eyes! I've gone blind. Help!

JO: Hang on!

(Jo pulls Mr Happy's head off. It is Dave Best.)

JO: *(Shocked)* Dave!

DAVE BEST: My eyes!

(Dave staggers out of the restaurant, rubbing his eyes. Monica comes back in with a kitchen knife. She heads towards Mr Moody.)

MONICA: Animals of the world, unite. Meat is murder!

MOODY: So's killing me! Help!

(Monica runs past Mr Moody and out of the restaurant. Mr Moody looks through the window.)

MOODY: *(In horror)* Oh no! Mr Rottenburger's here!

(Mr Moody races out of the restaurant. Jo, Jaz and Janice peer out of the window.)

JAZ: Look, Mr Rottenburger's getting out of the car.

JO: He doesn't look very happy.

JANICE: He's just seen all the customers being sick in the bushes.

JAZ: And all the children screaming at Mr Happy cos his head's come off.

JO: What's Monica doing?

JAZ: She's going to the bouncy castle. She's still got that knife.

JANICE: She won't, will she?

JO: Oh, she will.

(There is a large explosion from outside.)

JANICE: That's the first time I've ever seen a bouncy castle explode.

JAZ: It's blown Mr Happy right through Mr Rottenburger's windscreen.

JO: Oh look, poor Mr Moody. He's crying. Bless.

(There is a squeal of tyres from outside.)

JAZ: Mr Rottenburger didn't stay long, did he?

(Jaz, Jo and Janice wave through the window.)

JAZ, JO & JANICE: *(Together)* Have a nice day!

SCENE THREE

Later that evening. The restaurant is closed.

MOODY: My life is over.

JANICE: Come on, Mr Moody. It's not as bad as all that. You'll bounce back.

MOODY: Bounce! *(He bursts into tears.)*

(Janice comforts Mr Moody.)

JO: *(To Dave Best)* So, you're big in advertising, then?

DAVE BEST: Listen, Jo…

JO: So you haven't got a Ferrari.

DAVE BEST: No.

JO: And the house in London with the swimming pool?

DAVE BEST: I still live with me mum.

JO: Why did you pretend to be a big shot?

DAVE BEST: I didn't think you'd fancy me if I wasn't a big success. I was always top of the heap at college. But then I left and … things were different.

JANICE: Welcome to the real world.

DAVE BEST: I had to start again at the bottom, and since then it's been downhill all the way. It made me realise, I'm nothing special. I'm just an ordinary bloke.

JAZ: …who makes a living in a stupid costume.

DAVE BEST: It was the only job I could get. *(To Jo, hopefully)* And it *is* advertising.

JO: Yeah, right.

DAVE BEST: Will you still go out with me now you know the truth?

JO: No!

DAVE BEST: See? You won't go out with me because I'm a nobody.

JO: Wrong! I won't go out with you cos you lied to me.

JANICE: *I* was going to be somebody. I never bothered at school. Then I met Barry. Got married. Had kids.

JO: You could have gone back to college.

JANICE: Never had time. We needed the money. So, here I am.

JAZ: My dad wanted me to be a nuclear scientist.

(Janice stares at him in amazement.)

JAZ: He gave me a chemistry set once.

JANICE: Did you make anything with it?

JAZ: Ink. *(He takes a napkin and starts to draw.)*

JO: Don't be so miserable! We've all still got jobs …

MOODY: You haven't! You brought that Monica here! You're sacked!

JO: *(Taken aback)* Oh! Well, it was a rotten job anyway.

MOODY: None of us'll have jobs soon. Not after today.

(A buzzer sounds. Janice goes to the door.)

MOODY: Tell them we're closed! Probably forever!

JO: It's not a customer. It's a motorbike delivery man.

JANICE: *(Coming back in)* It's from head office, Mr Moody.

MOODY: Oh God. This is it. Our marching orders. I've grilled my last Cheesy Woppa. *(He breaks down.)*

JANICE: Shall I read it, then?

(Mr Moody signals Janice to carry on. She opens the envelope. Her face breaks into a huge grin.)

JANICE: It's not the sack! They've made us Crew of the Month!

JO, JAZ & MOODY: *(Together)* What?!

(Mr Moody snatches the letter and reads it.)

JANICE: It's the competition – to find a name for the new kangaroo burger. Jo's won it.

JO: I only filled the form in for a laugh!

JAZ: What did you call it?

JO: A Mister Hoppy!

(Jaz takes a new napkin and starts to draw.)

MOODY: They want to use the name – and Jo's slogan as well! This calls for a celebration – shakes all round!

(Janice goes into the kitchen to make shakes.)

JO: What are you drawing, Jaz?

JAZ: I just got an idea – what do you think?

(He shows the doodle – it is a kangaroo with a big grin.)

MOODY: Brilliant! This is brilliant!

JAZ: Is it?

MOODY: *(Excited)* That *is* Mister Hoppy! *(He snatches the napkin from Jaz)* Wait until head office see this!

JO: See, Jaz, who said drawing would never get you anywhere? And Dave – you can be Mister Hoppy!

DAVE BEST: Hoppy, hoppy, hoppy!

(Janice comes back in with a tray of shakes. All take one.)

MOODY: Ladies and gentlemen, a toast. Raise your maxi-shakes, please. This is a new dawn for Happy Burgers. A new era ... a new burger ... a new slogan:

ALL: *(In Australian accents)* Have a g'day!

(Blackout.)